illustrated exclusively for Blue Star
Jared Wright

Take a Hike

An Outdoor Coloring Adventure

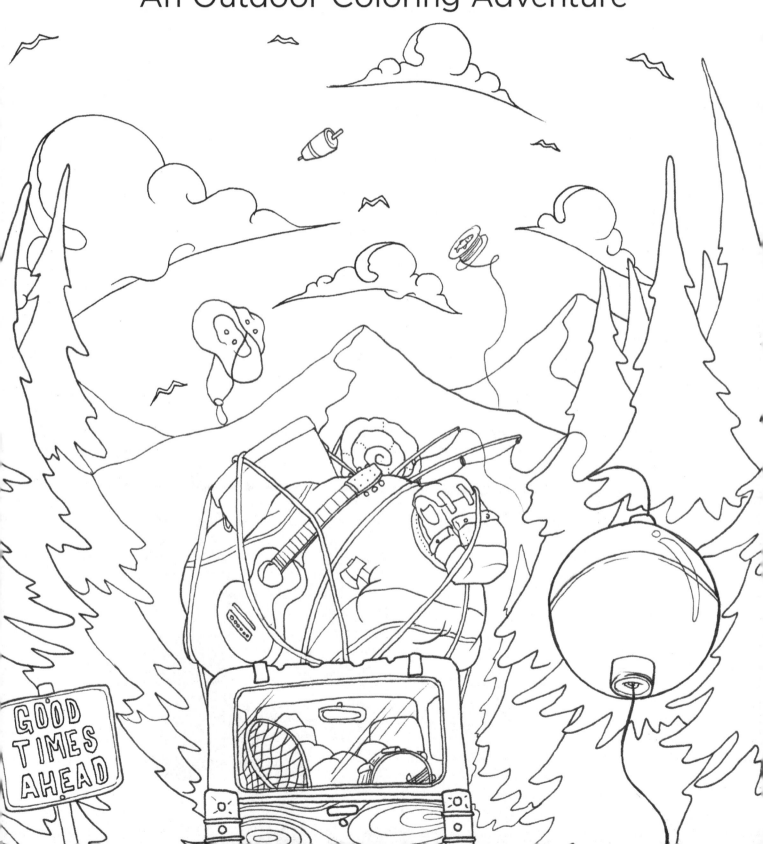

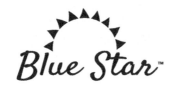

Teamwork makes the dream work

....

Illustrator
Jared Wright

....

Design & Production
Chris Ramirez
Tommy Barros
JP Garrigues
Peter Licalzi

Publishing & Operations
Brenna Dominguez
Clare Burch
Kiersten Blair
Reagan Lewis
Camden Hendricks

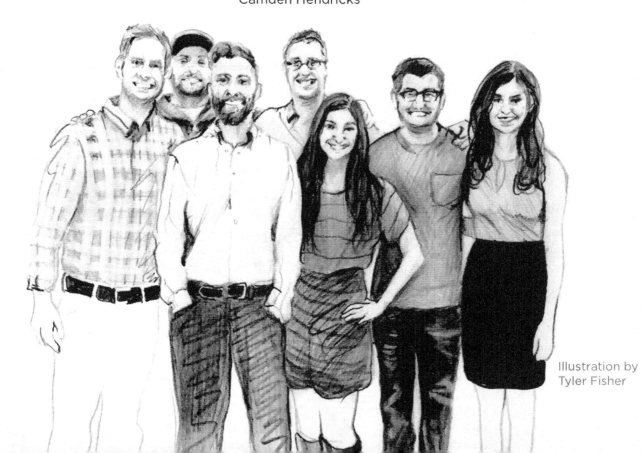

Illustration by
Tyler Fisher

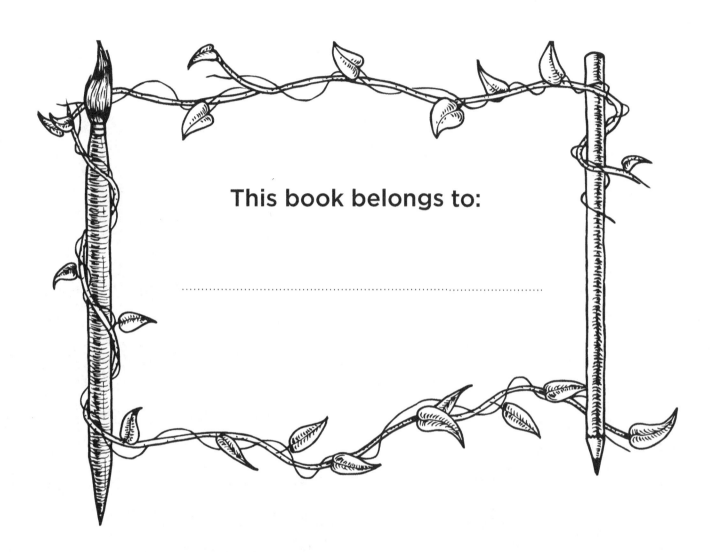

This book belongs to:

....

Show us your art...
We'll show the world.

/bluestarcoloring

for free prints, updates, & more visit
bluestarcoloring.com

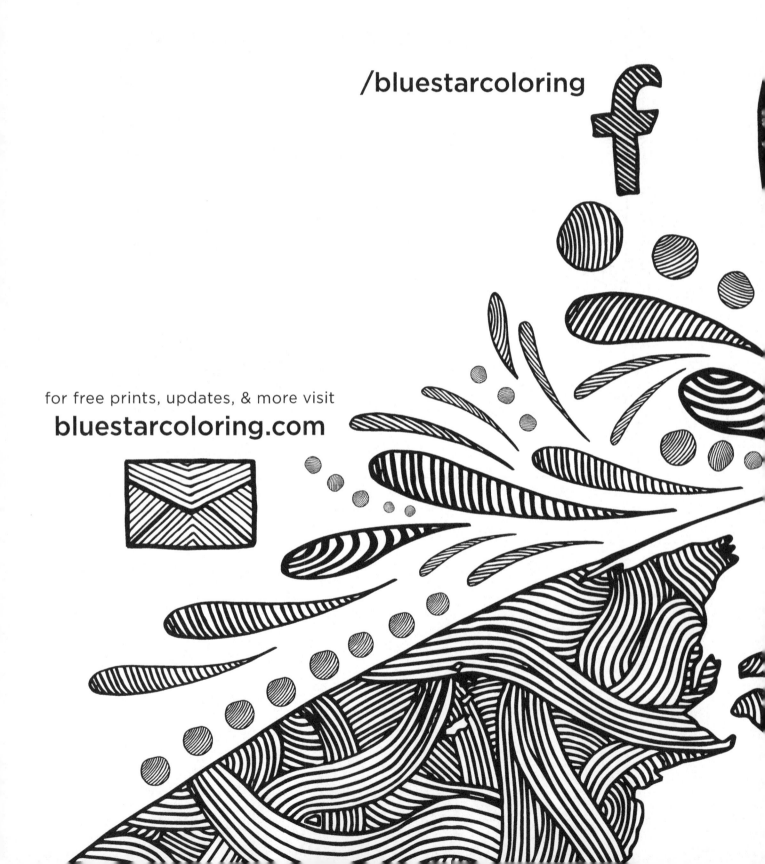

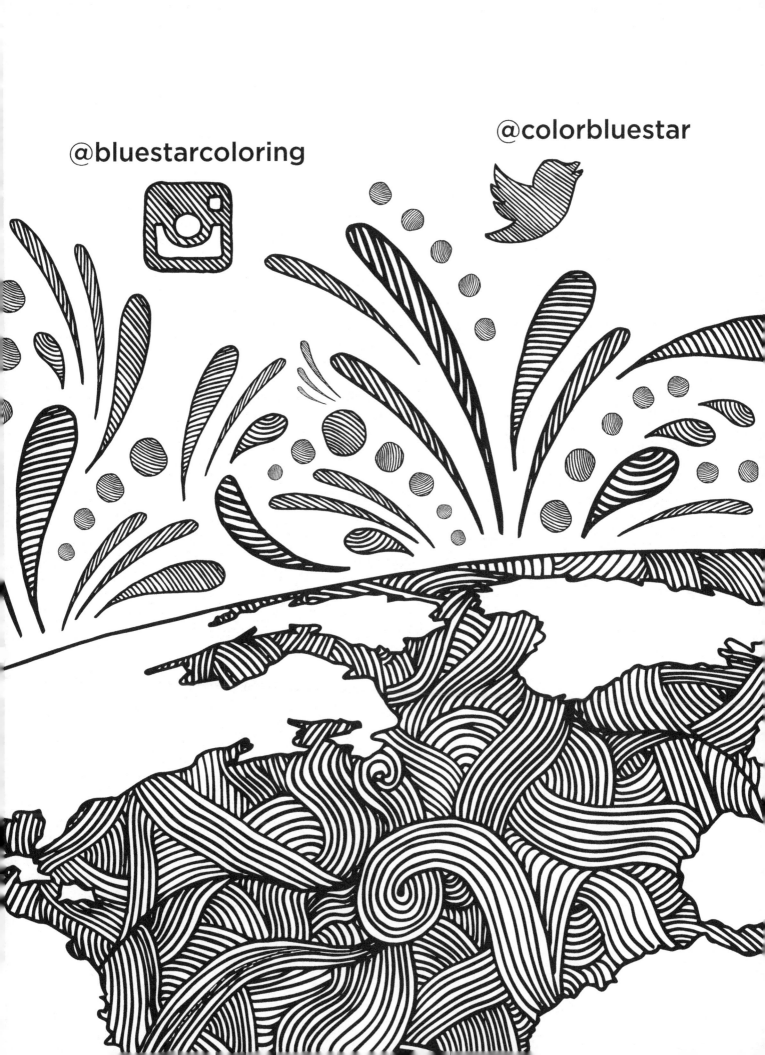

@bluestarcoloring

@colorbluestar

We'll never be perfect, but that won't stop us from trying. Your feedback makes us a better company. We want your ideas, criticism, compliments or anything else you think we should hear!

Oh, and if you don't love this coloring book, we'll refund your money immediately. No questions asked.

Send anything and everything to contact@bluestarcoloring.com.

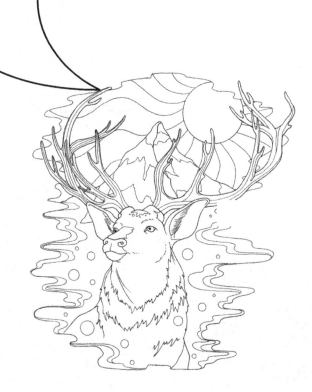

How to Use This Book

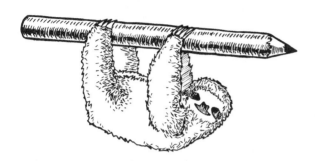

1 Break out your crayons or colored pencils.

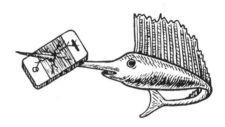

2 Turn off your phone, tablet, computer, whatever.

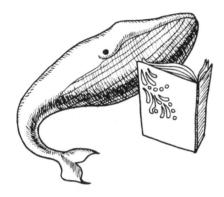

3 Find your favorite page in the book. That is the beginning.

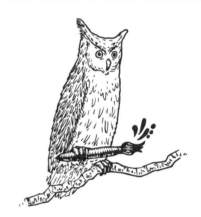

4 Start coloring.

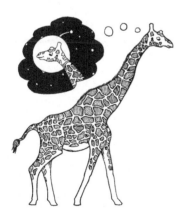

5 If you notice at any point that you are forgetting your worries, daydreaming freely or feeling more creative, curious, excitable, delighted, relaxed or any combination thereof, take a deep breath and enjoy it. Remind yourself that coloring, like dancing or falling in love, does not have a point. It is the point.

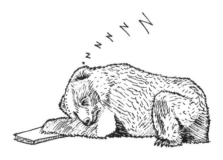

6 When you don't feel like it anymore, stop.

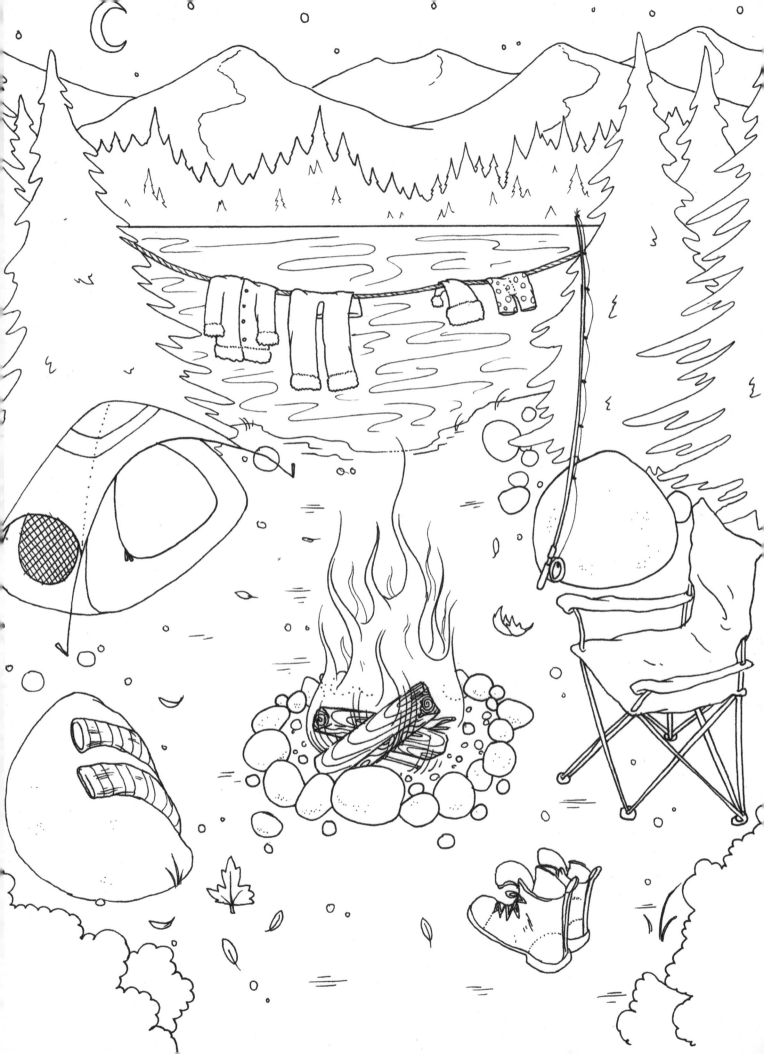

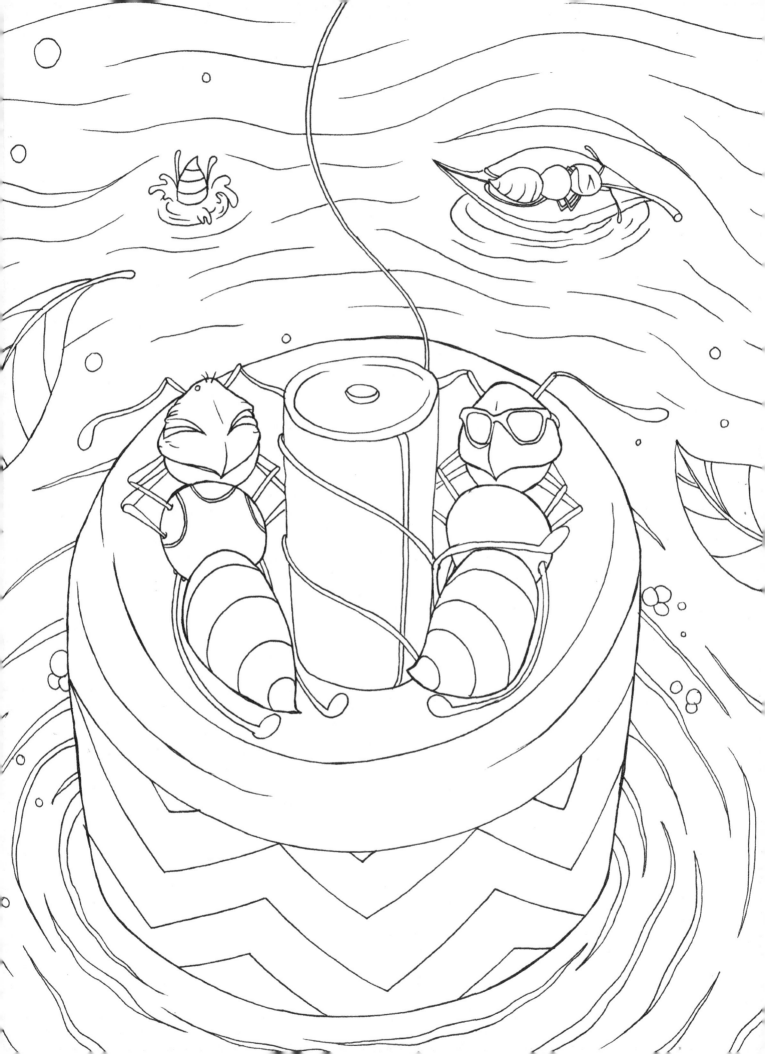

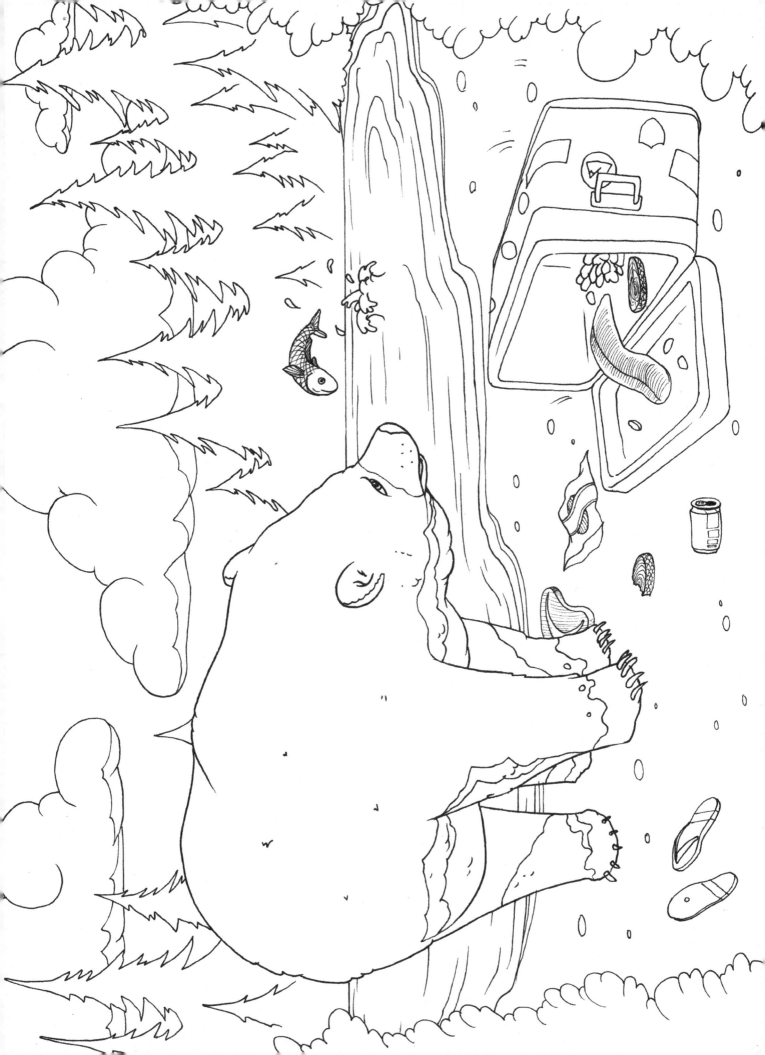

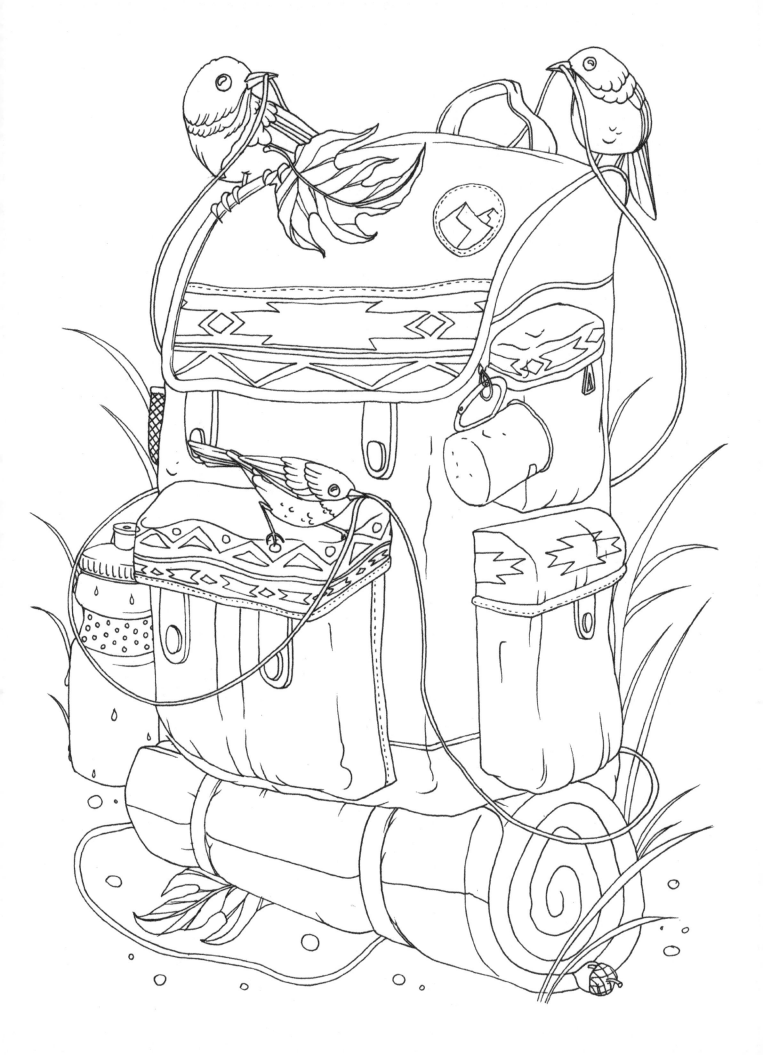

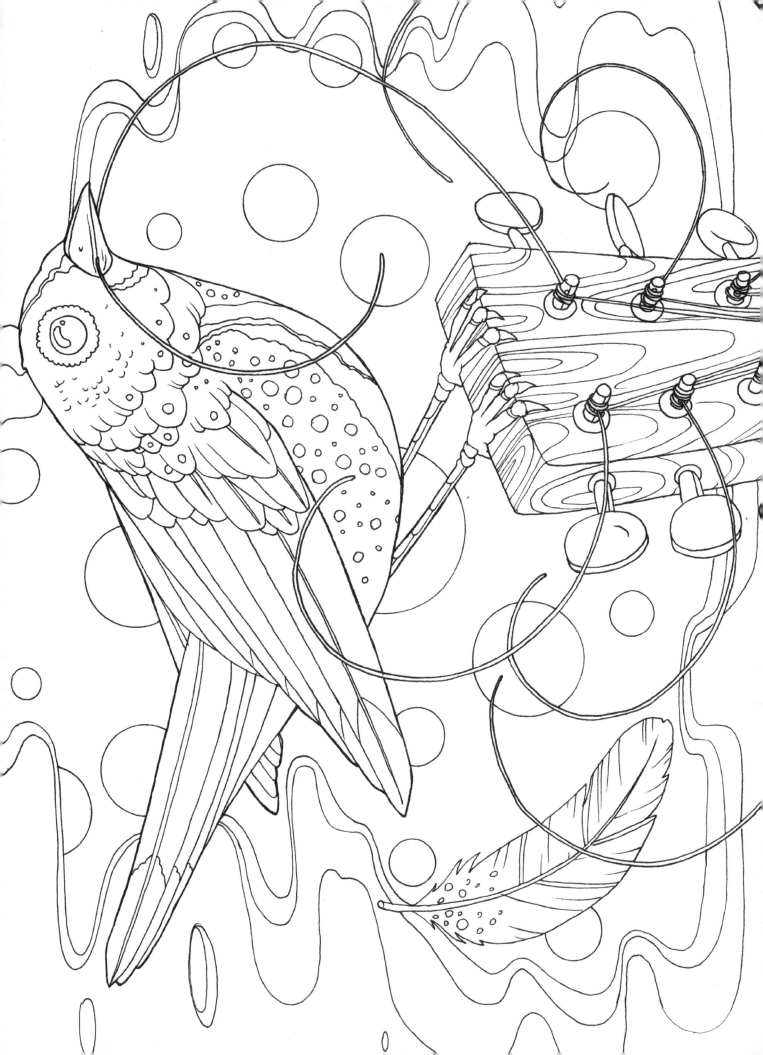

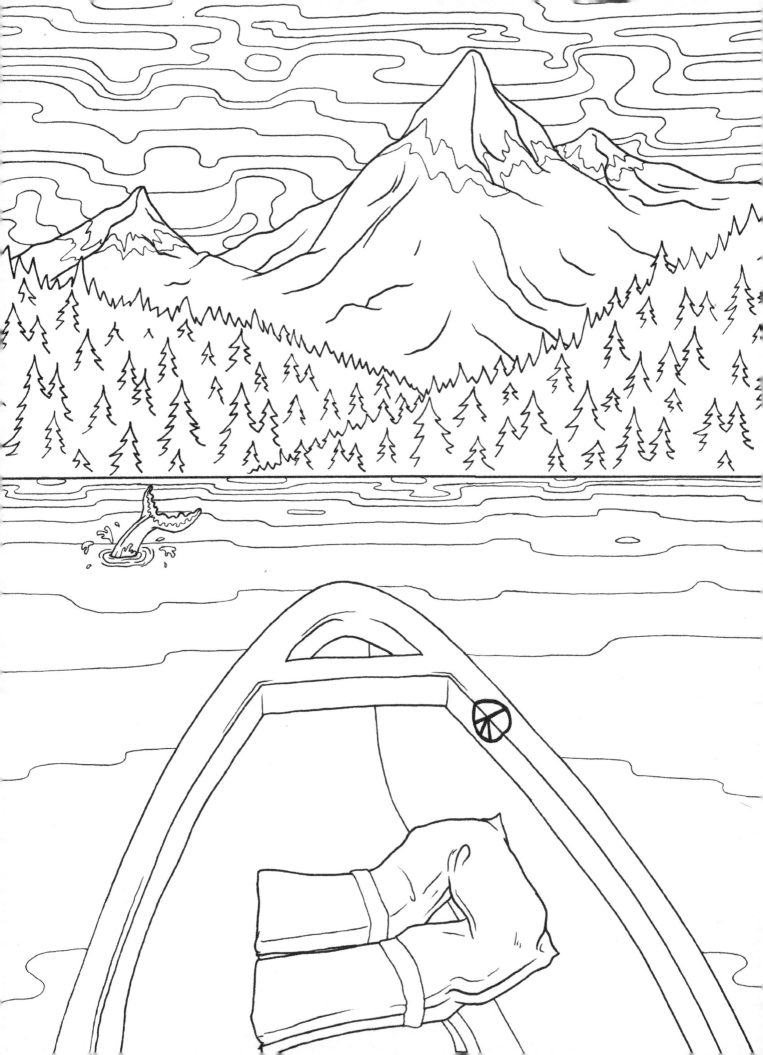

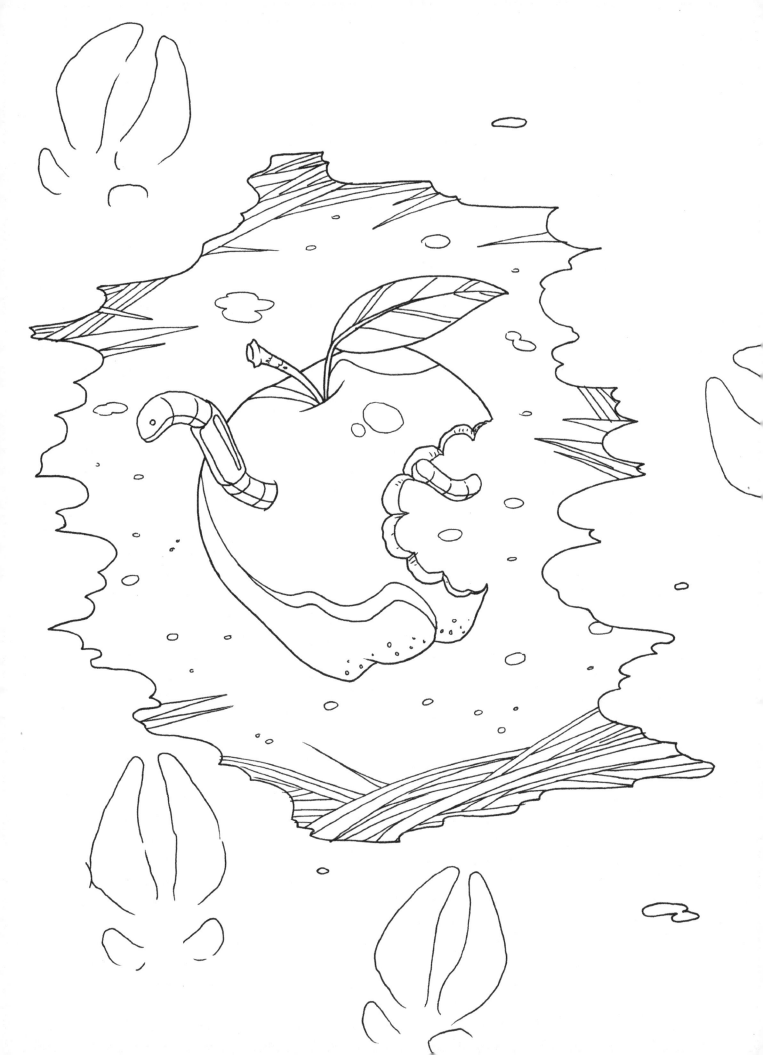

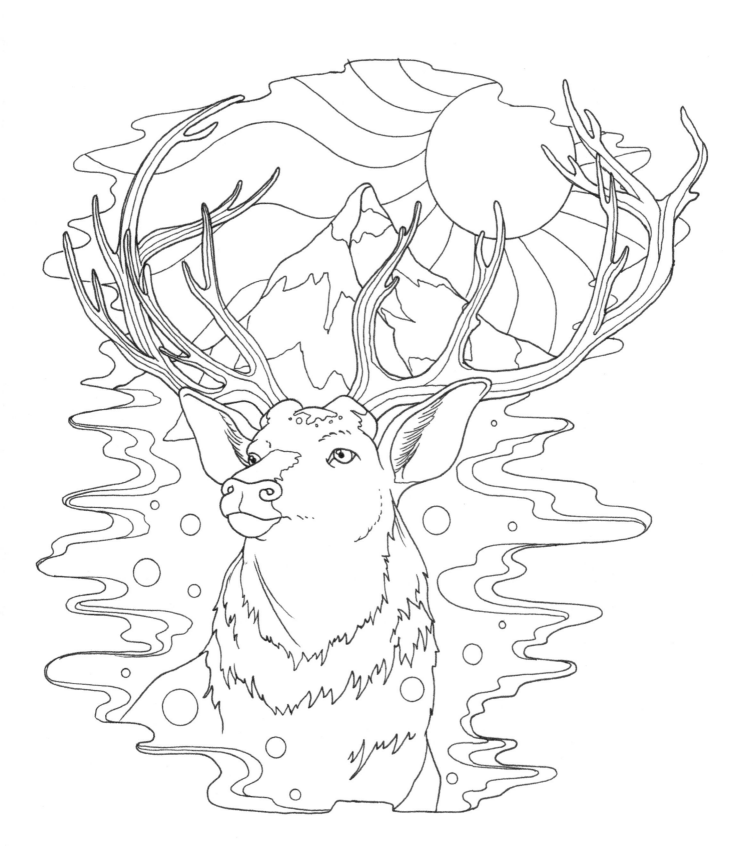

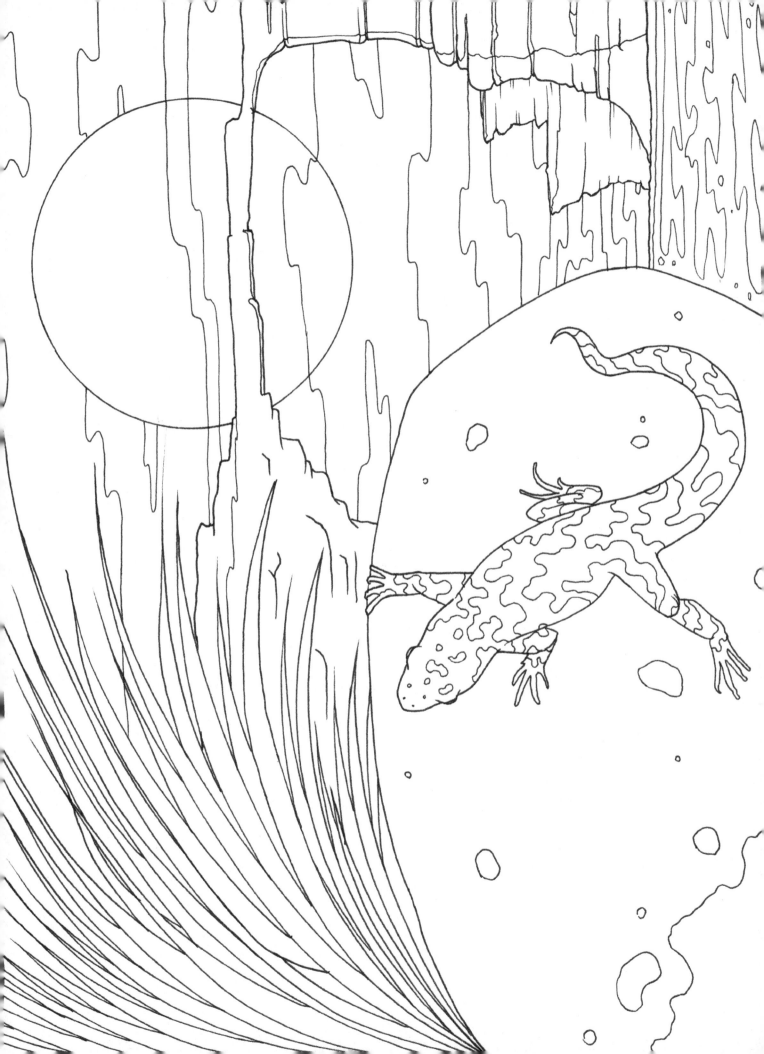

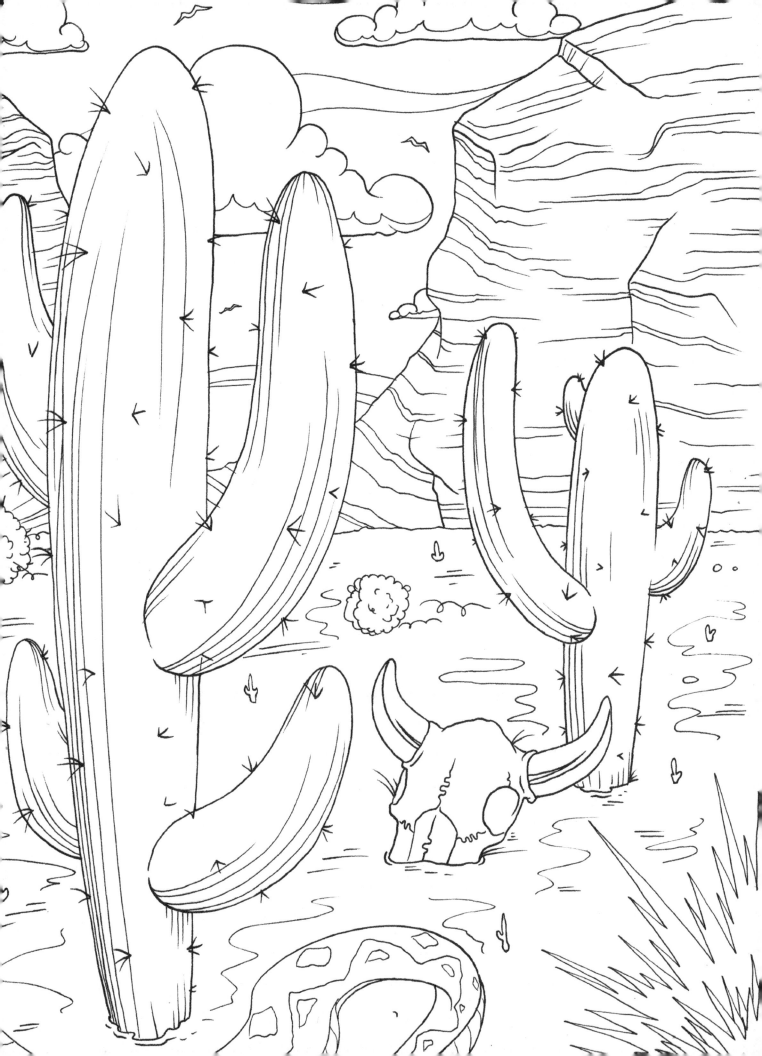

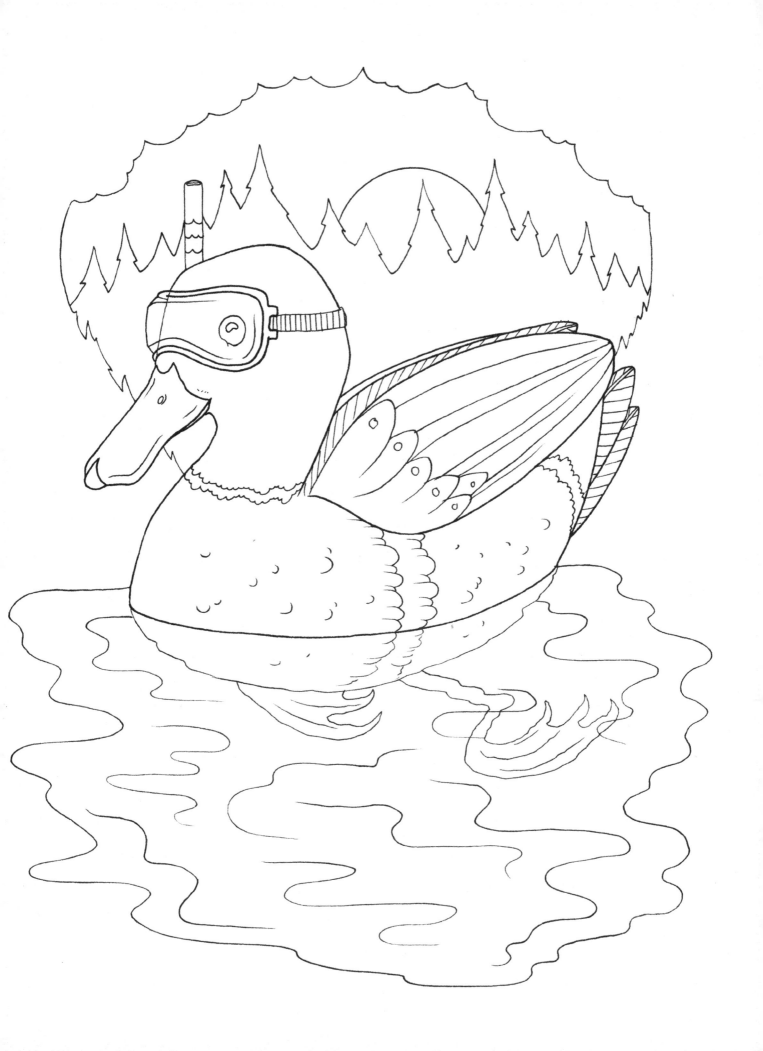

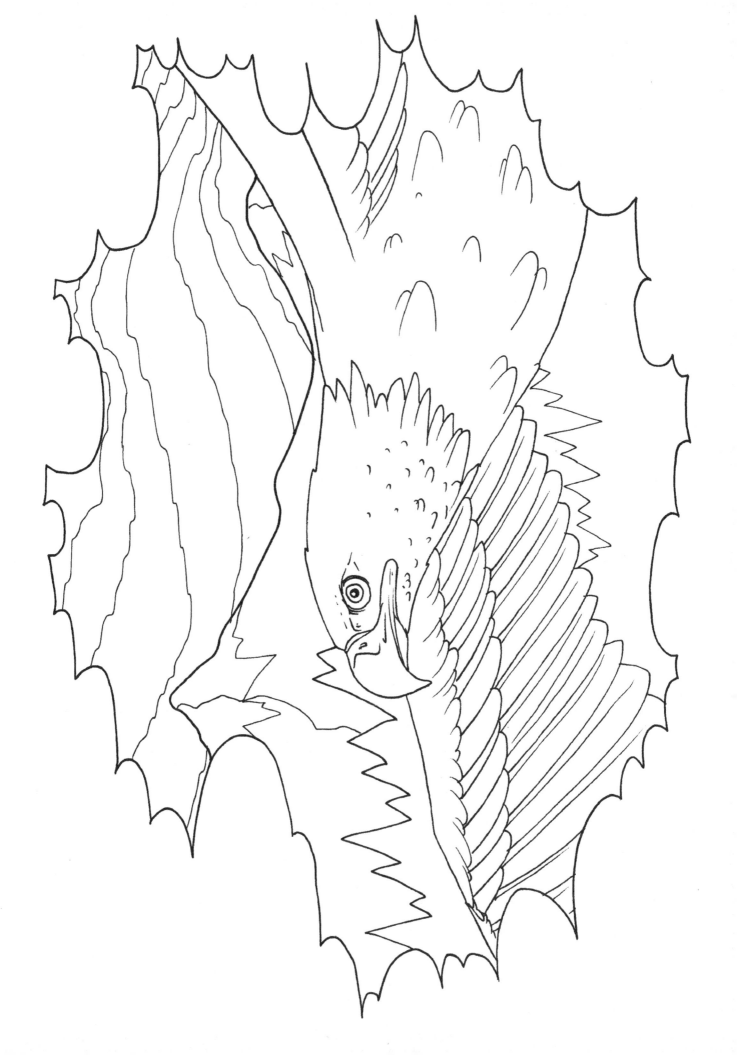

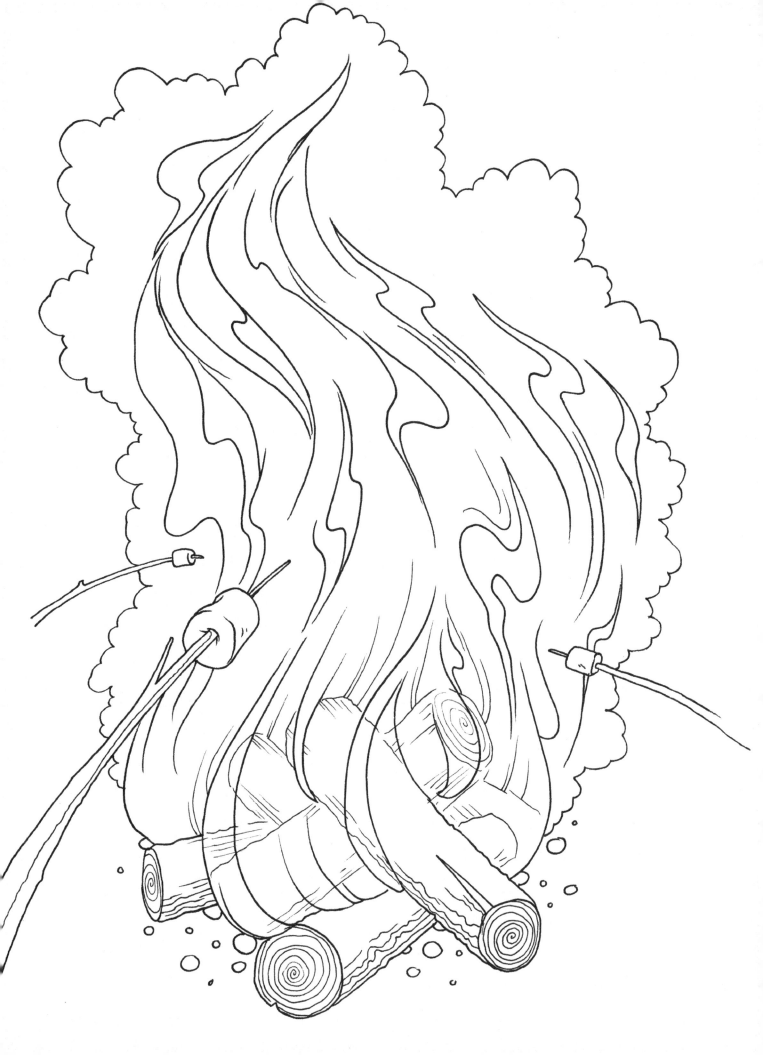

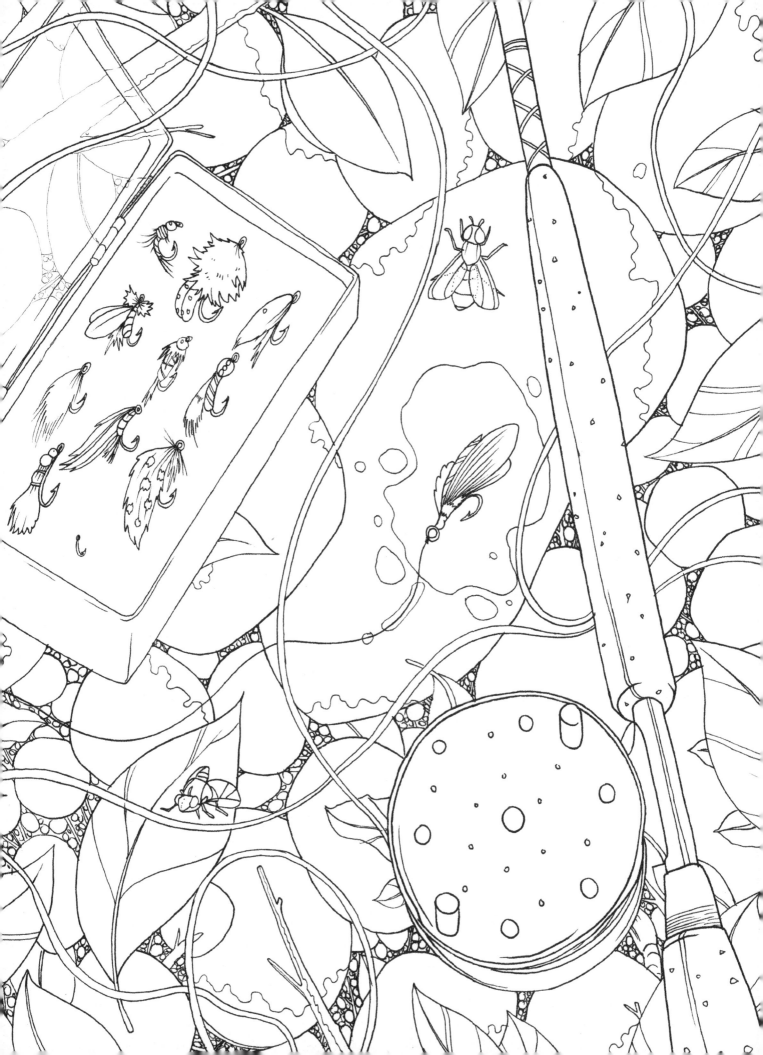

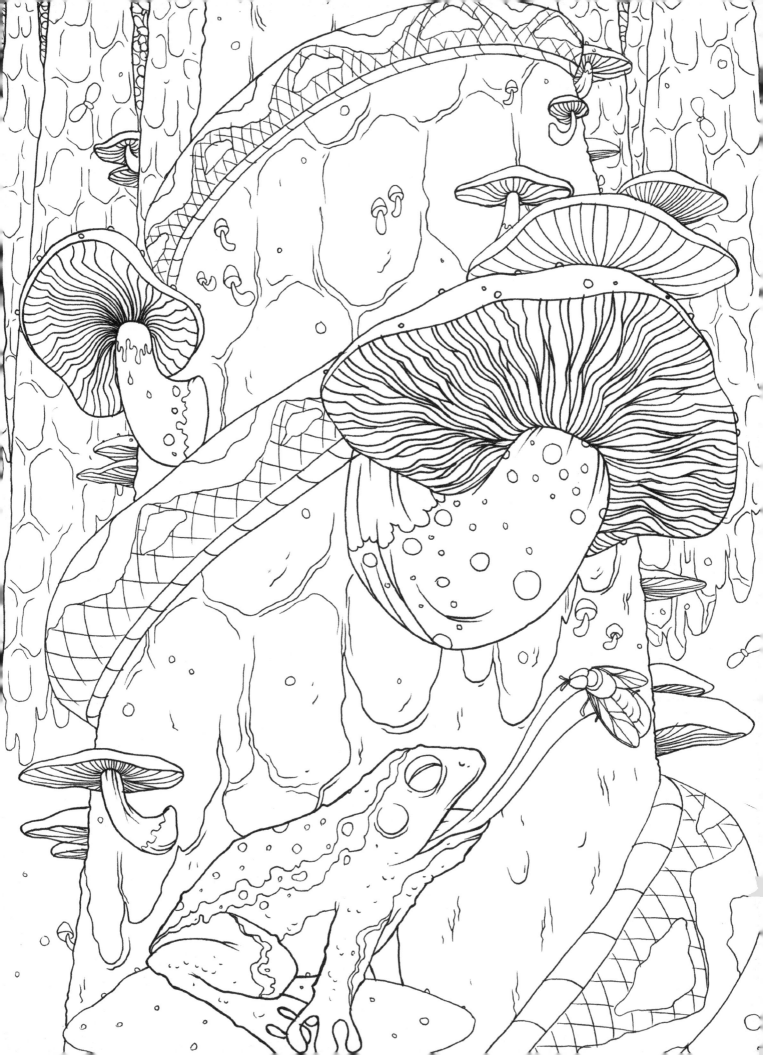

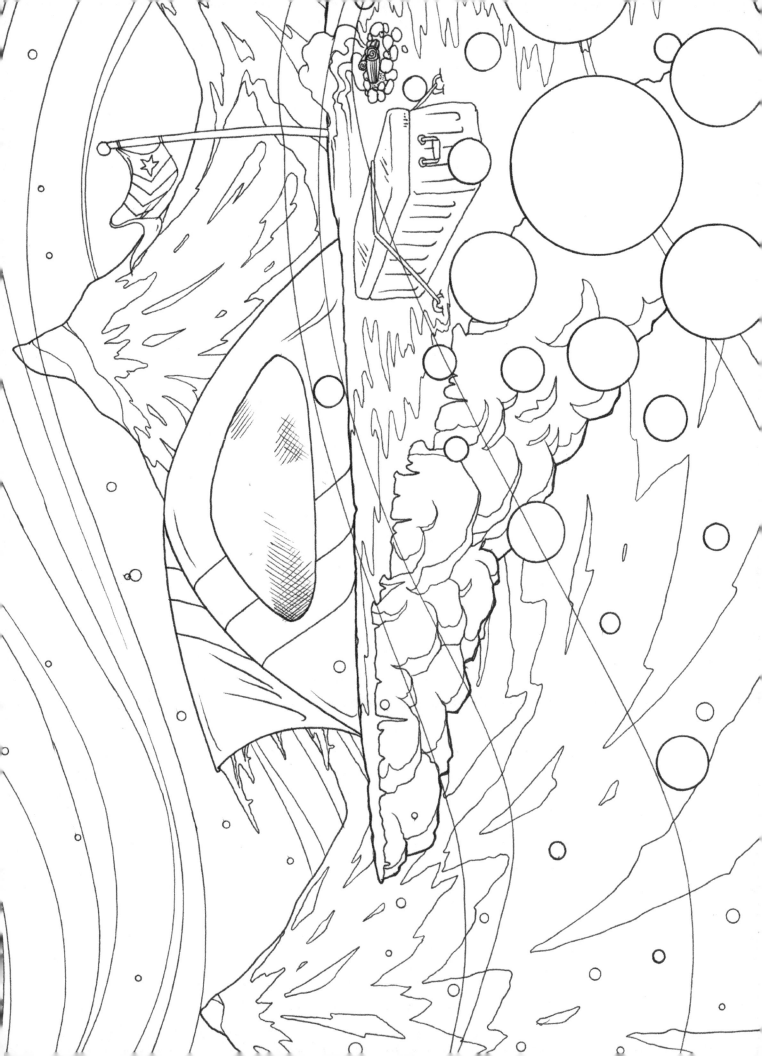

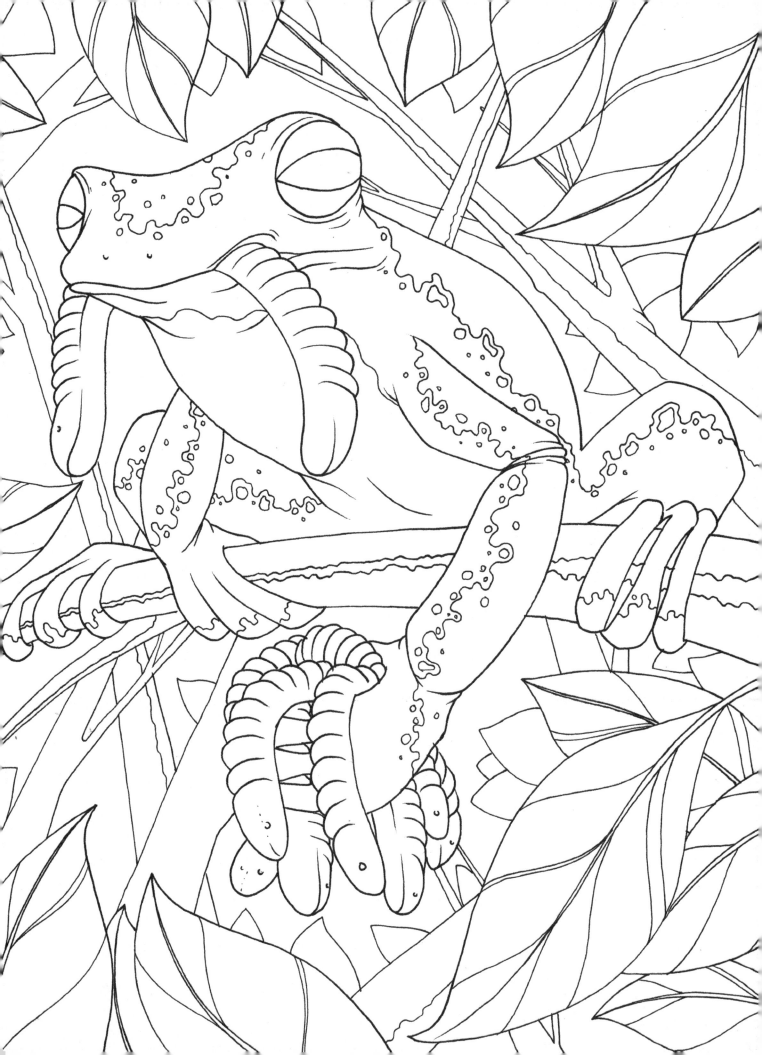

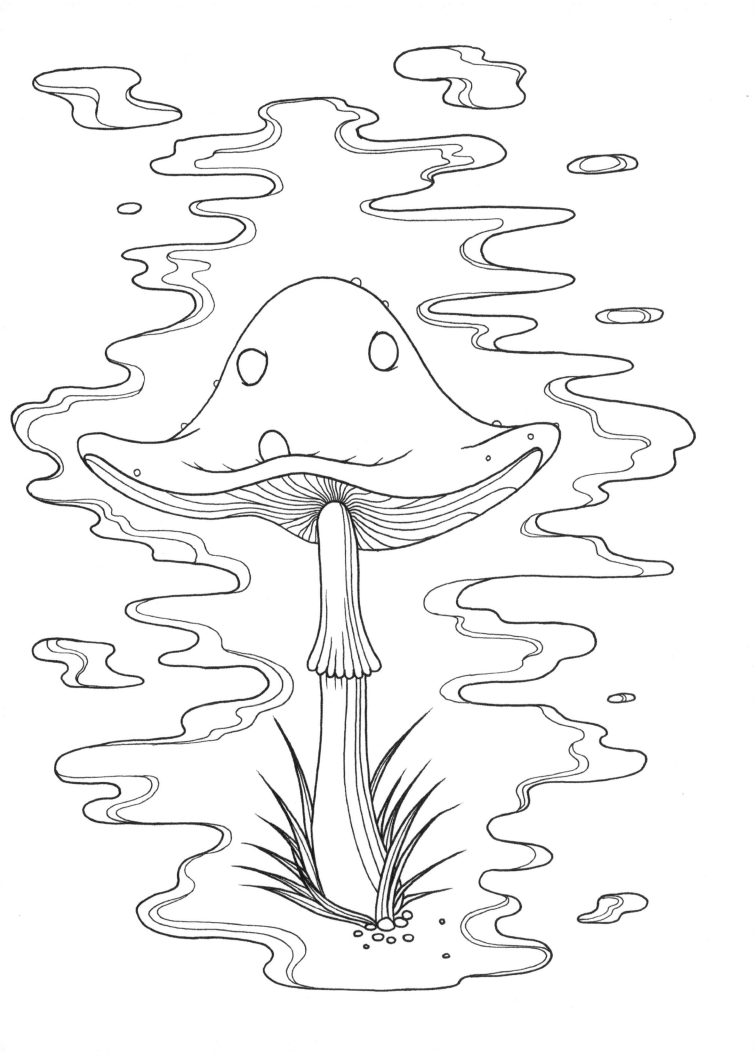

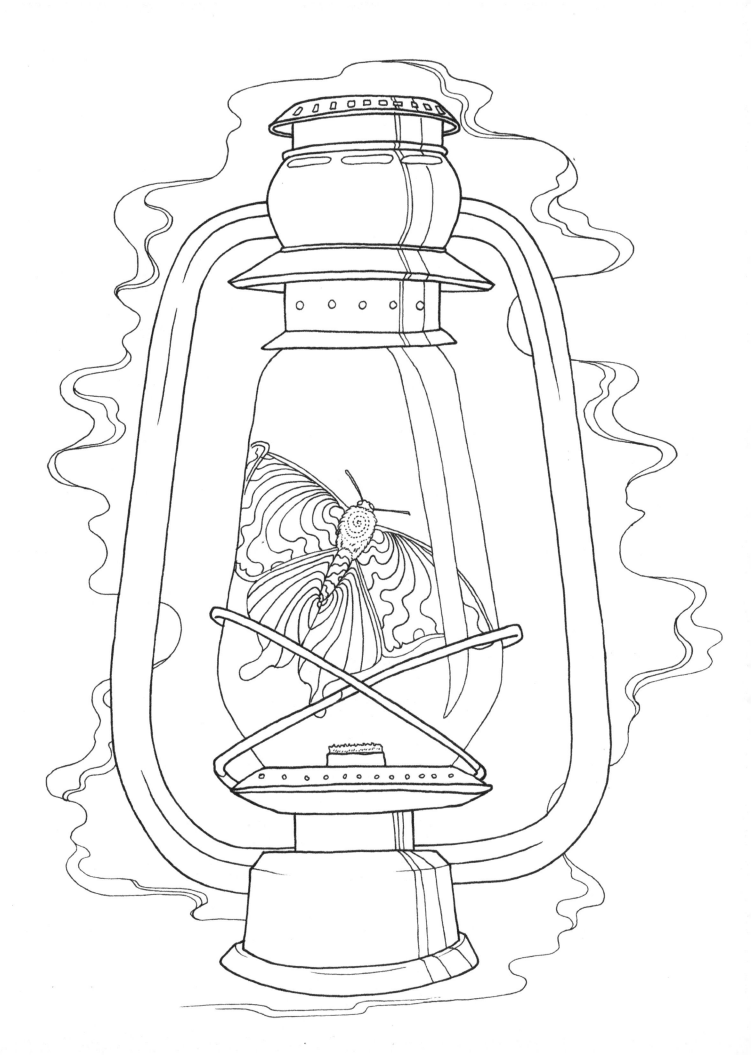

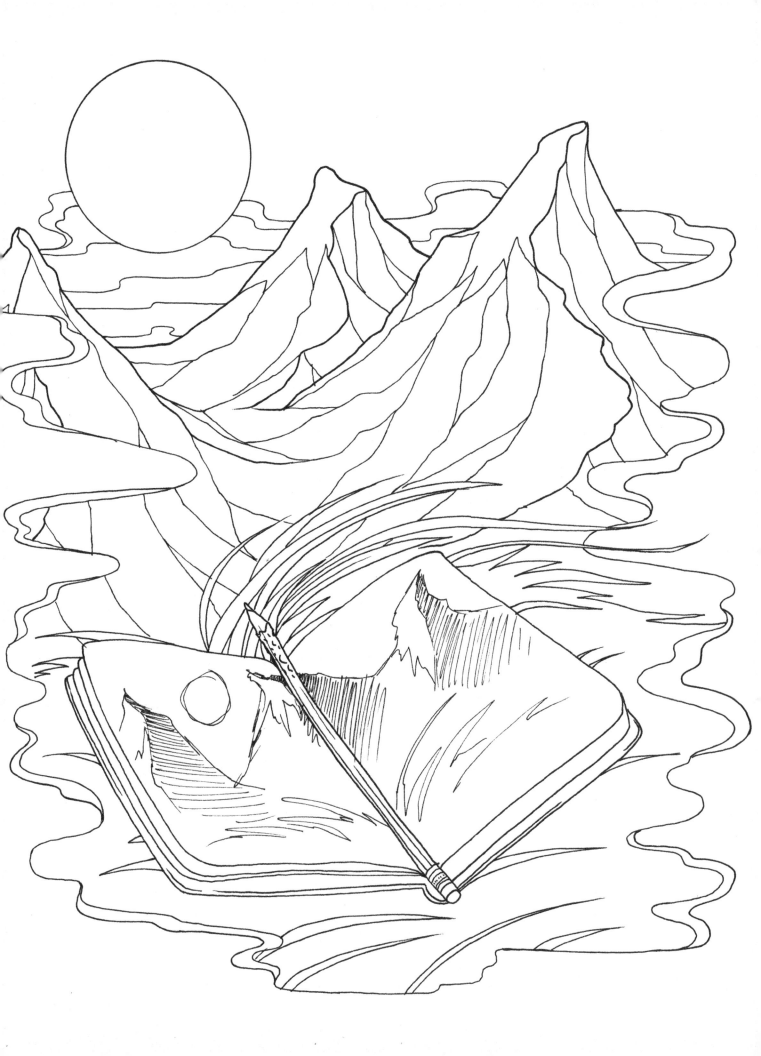

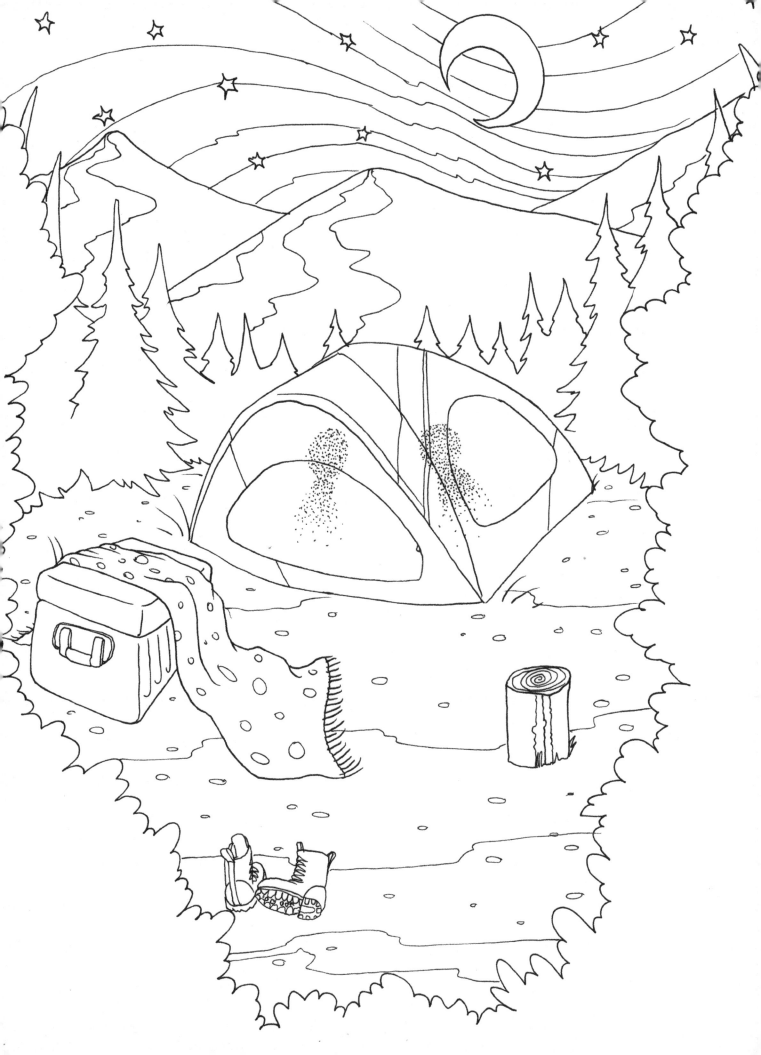

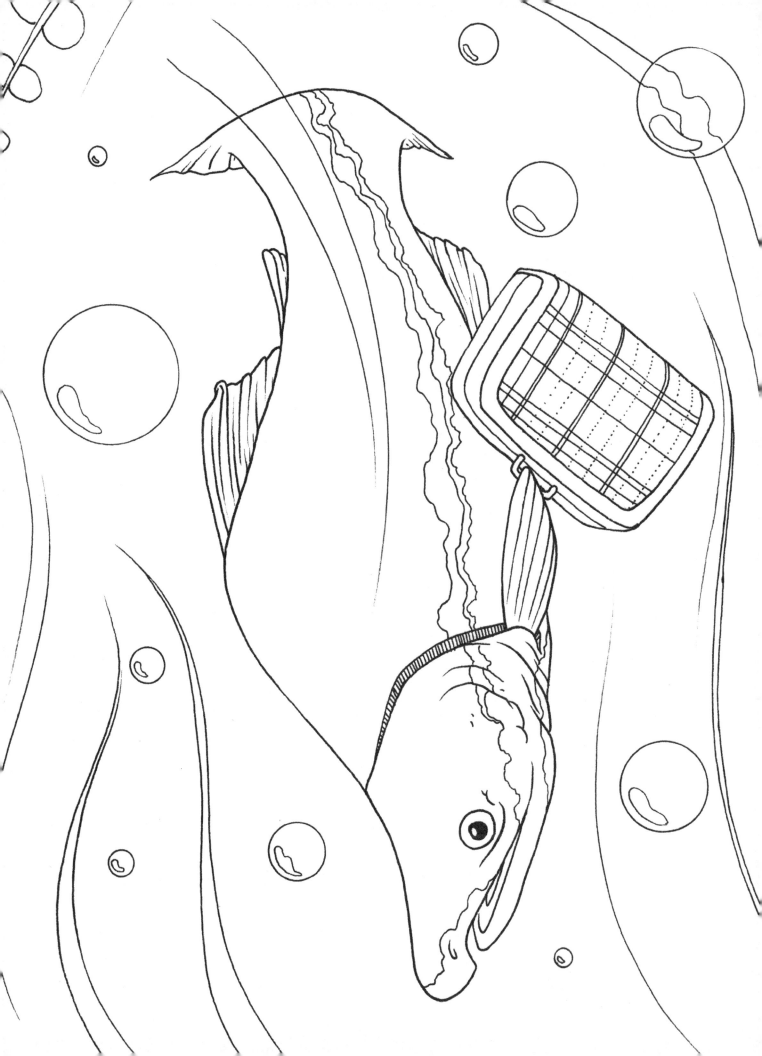

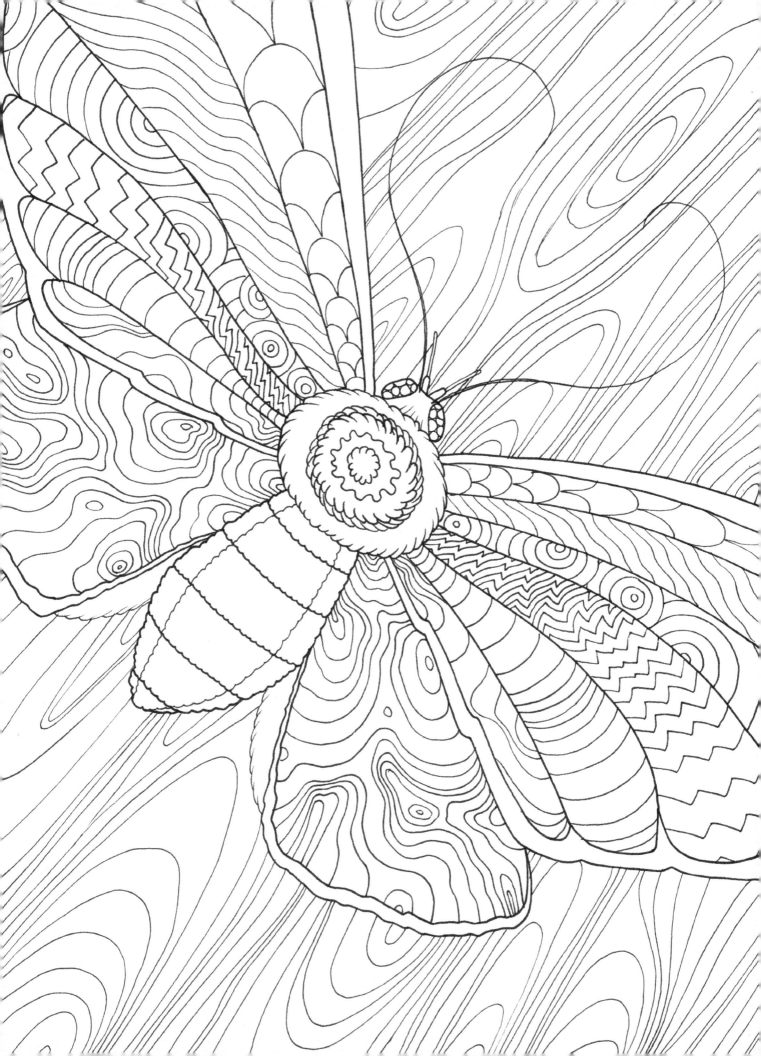

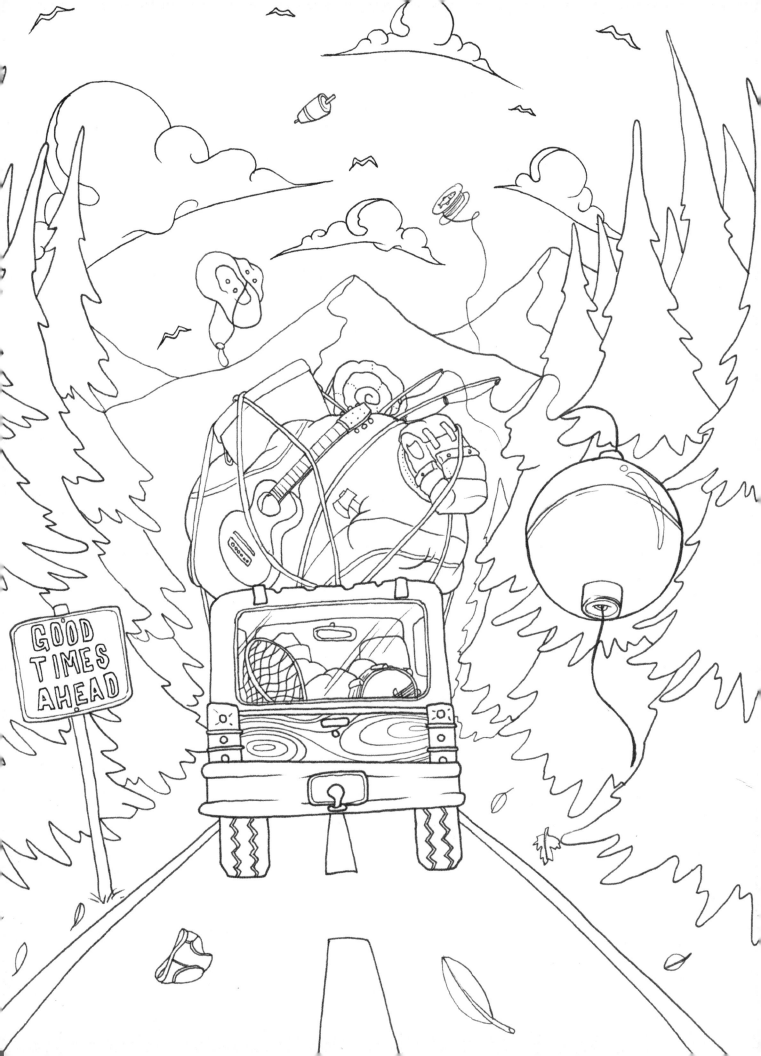

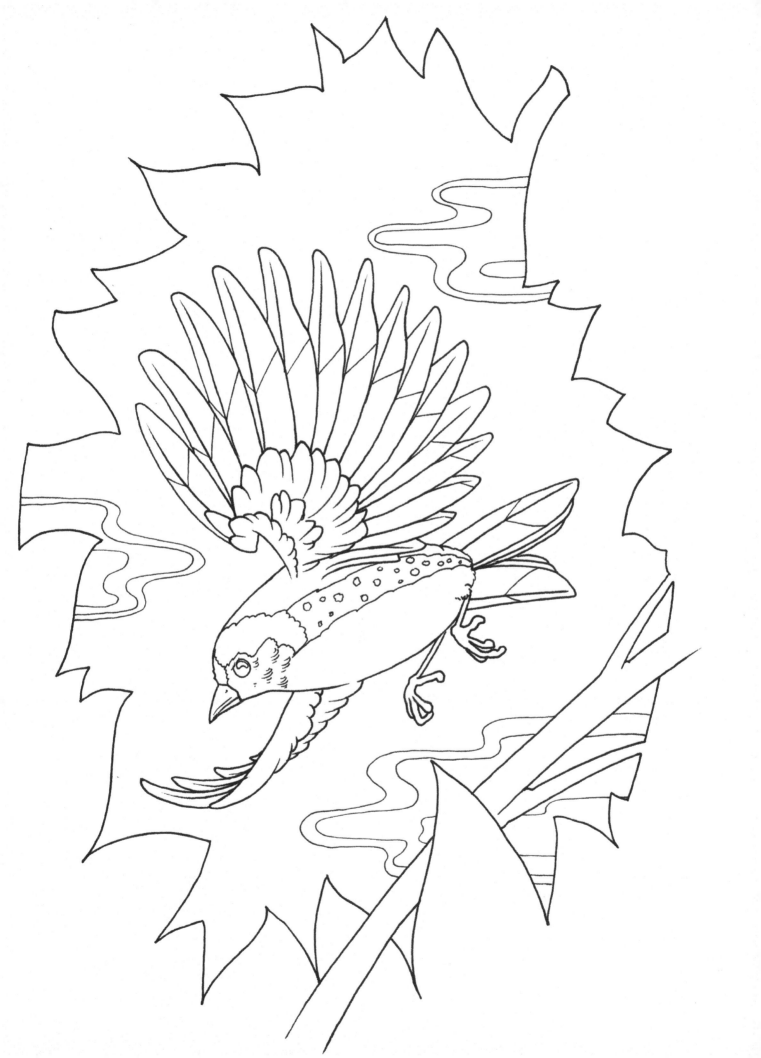

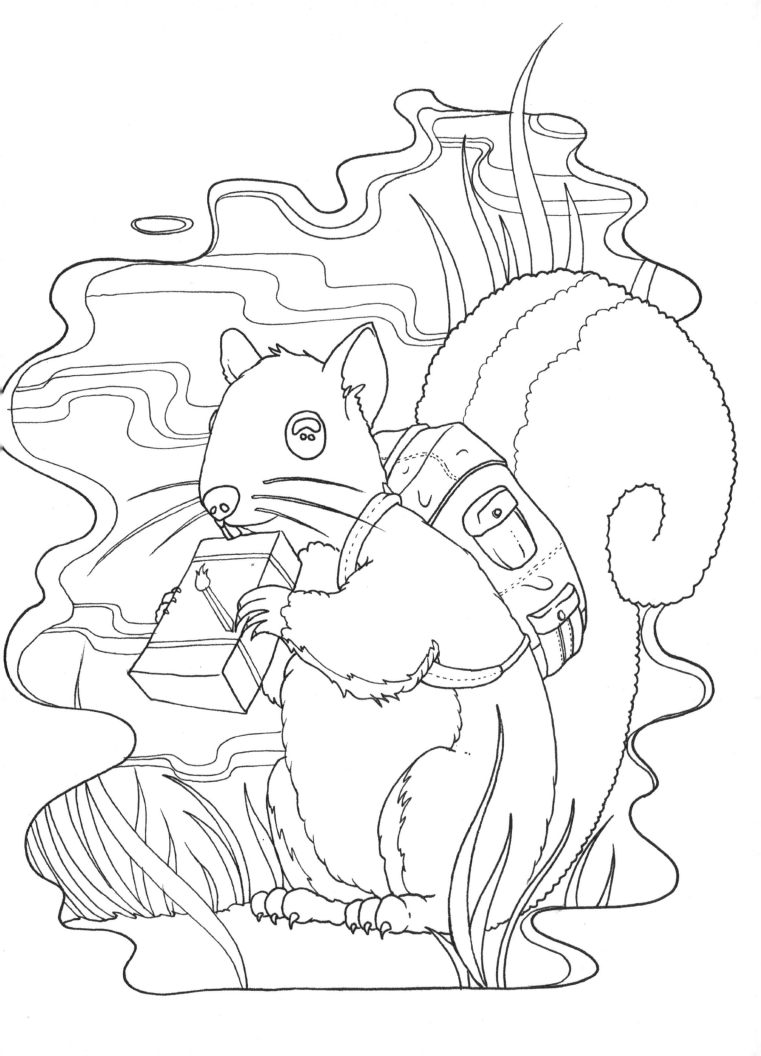

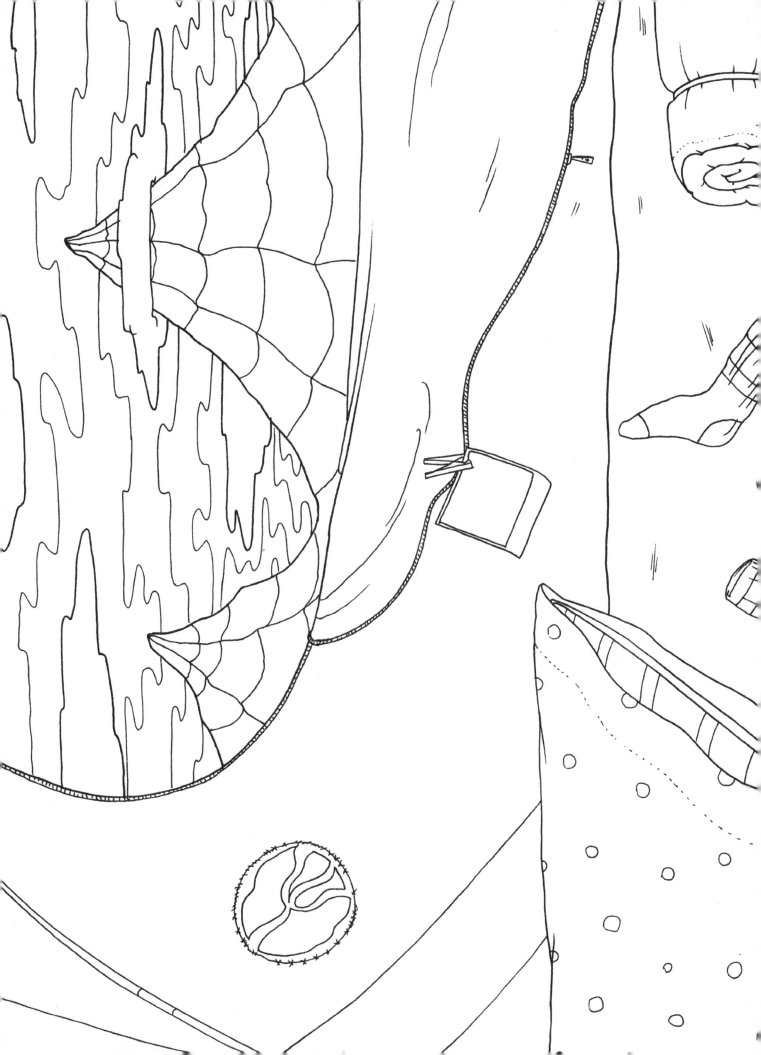

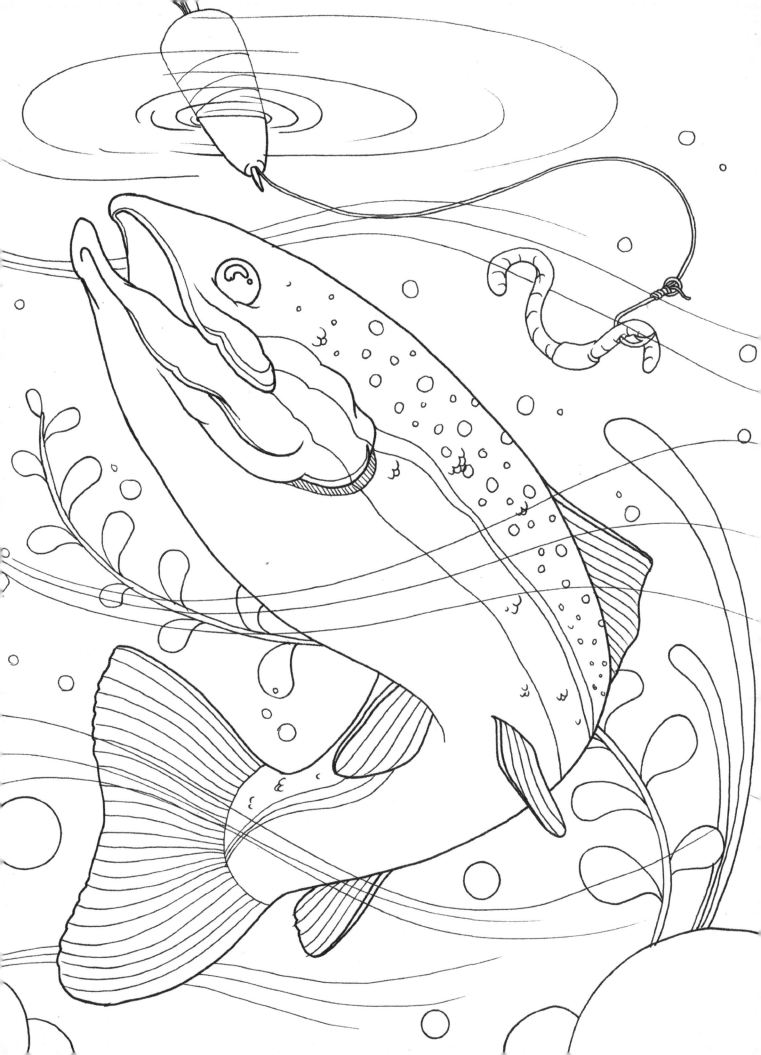

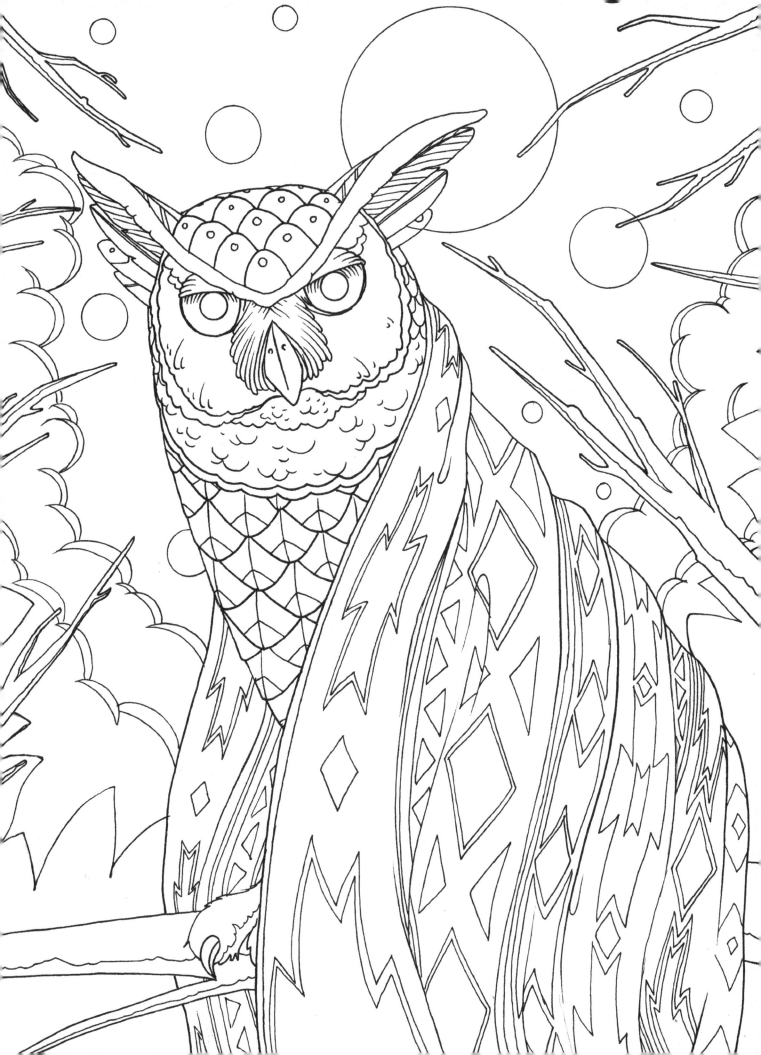

Bonus Images!

The following images are designs from other
Blue Star Coloring books. We hope you enjoy!

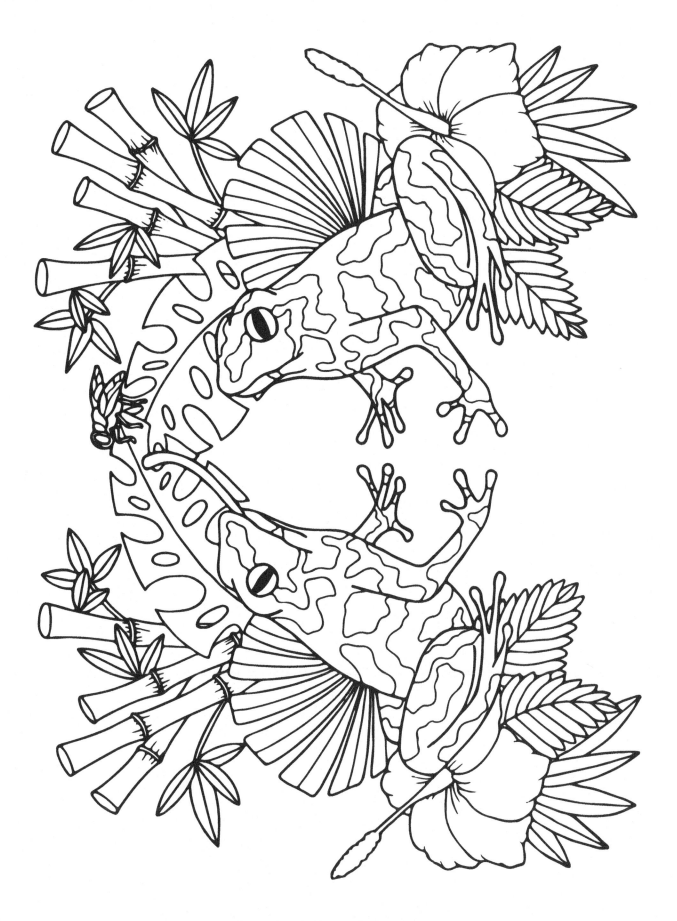

Tropical Travel Patterns
by Jaimie Horan

bluestarcoloring.com

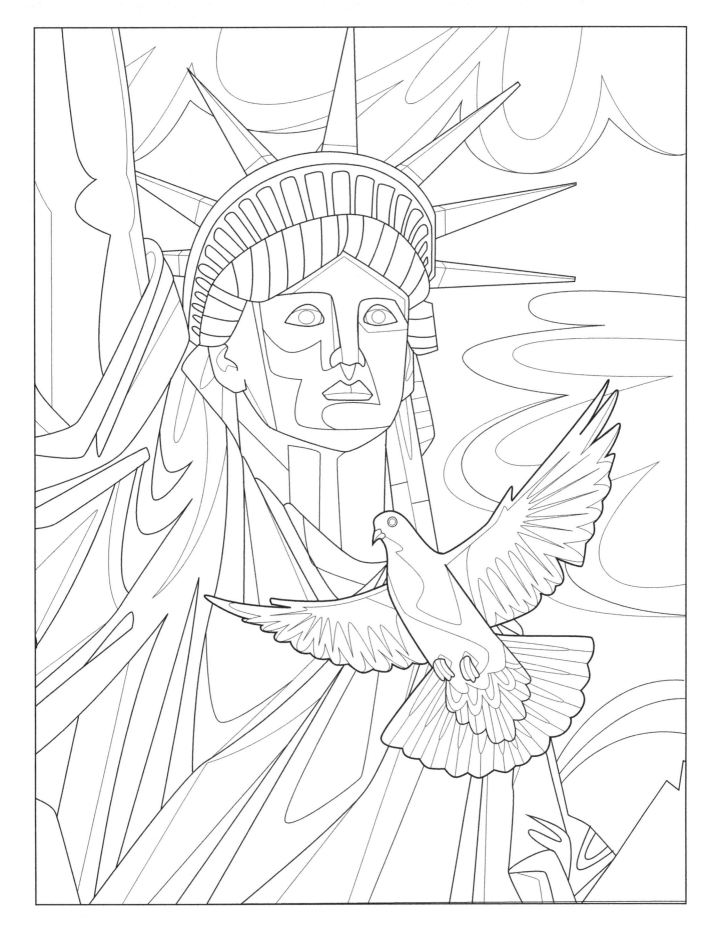

Birds of the World
by Rémy Simard

bluestarcoloring.com

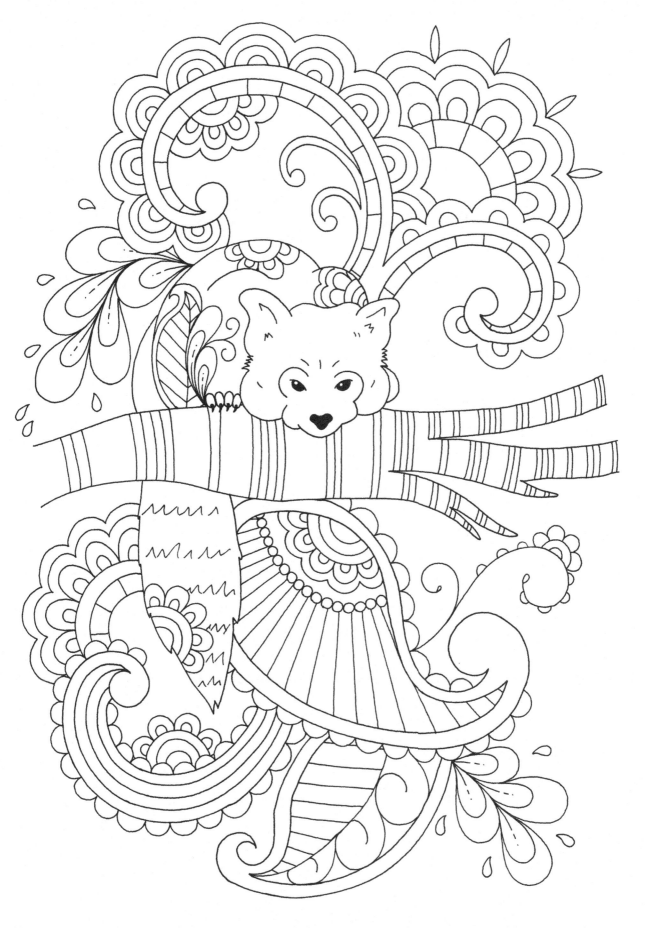

Exotic Animal Designs
by Katie Packer

bluestarcoloring.com

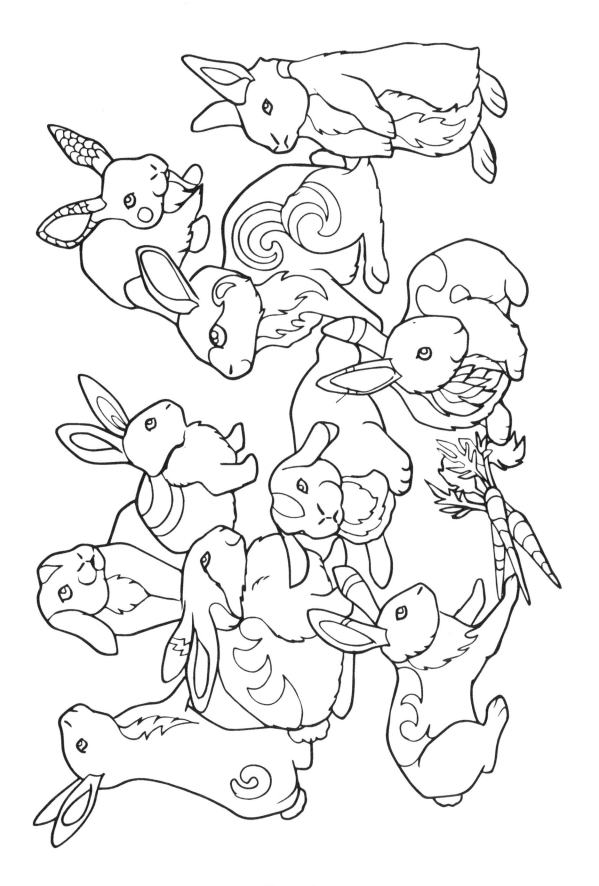

Bunnies

for Blue Star Inspire

by Katy Lipscomb

bluestarinspire.com

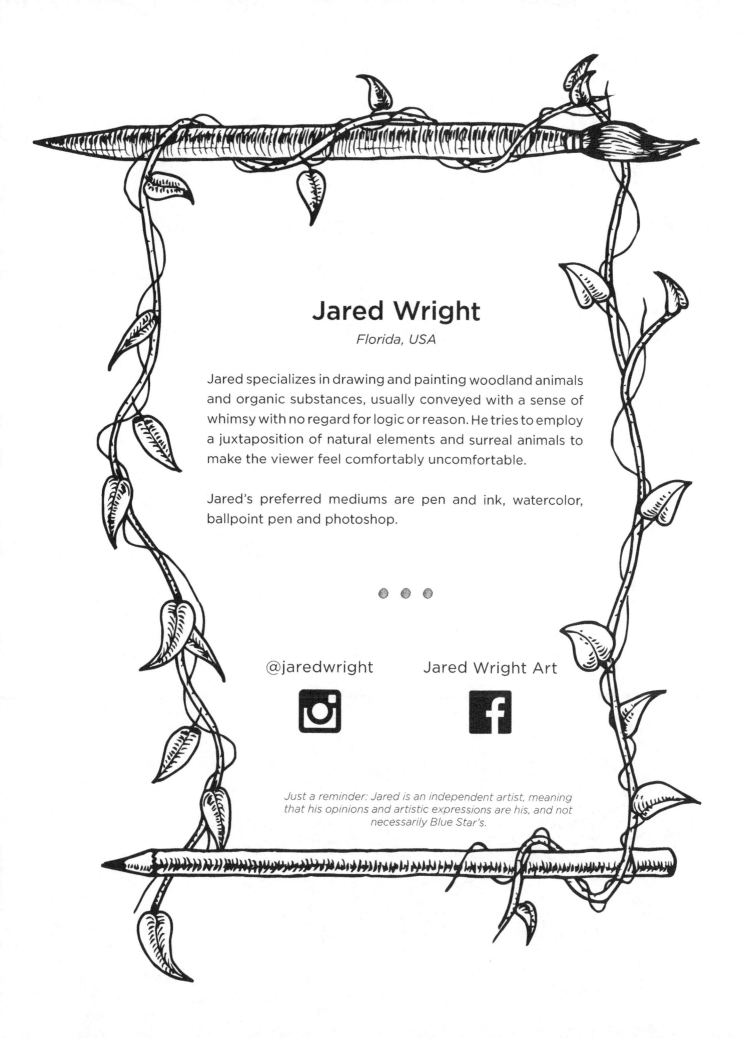

Jared Wright

Florida, USA

Jared specializes in drawing and painting woodland animals and organic substances, usually conveyed with a sense of whimsy with no regard for logic or reason. He tries to employ a juxtaposition of natural elements and surreal animals to make the viewer feel comfortably uncomfortable.

Jared's preferred mediums are pen and ink, watercolor, ballpoint pen and photoshop.

• • •

@jaredwright   Jared Wright Art

Just a reminder: Jared is an independent artist, meaning that his opinions and artistic expressions are his, and not necessarily Blue Star's.

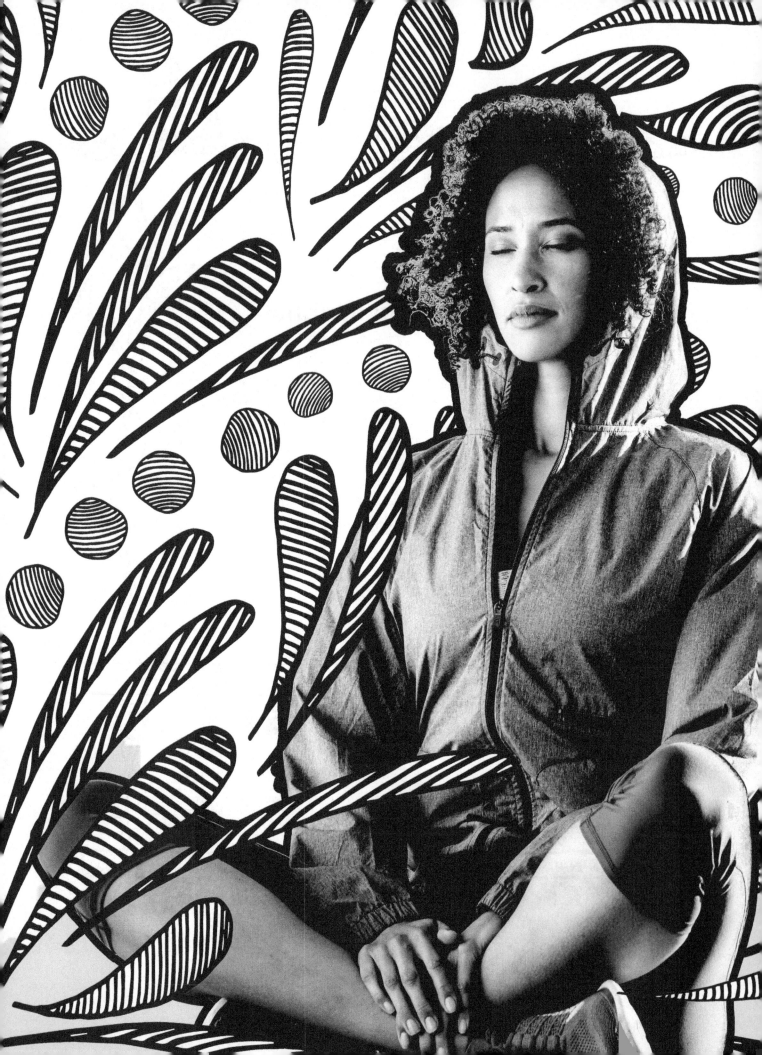

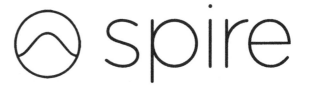

Find Your Calm with
Blue Star Coloring + Spire

Discover the mindfulness + activity tracker that helps you be calm – everywhere you go. Blue Star Coloring and Spire have partnered to bring you tranquility in all facets of life. Use Spire to track your state of mind – and when things get a little tense, pick up a Blue Star Coloring book to wind down, refocus, and bring energy back into your day.

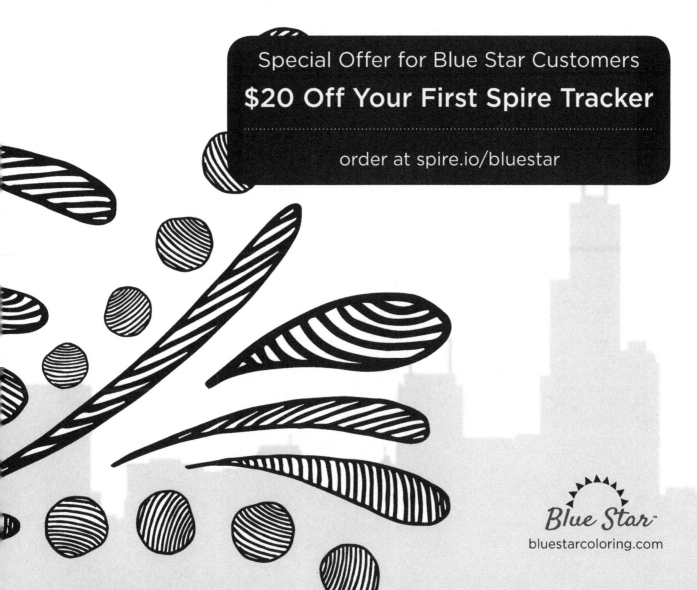

Blue Star™
bluestarcoloring.com

Made in the USA
Coppell, TX
22 April 2021

54331727R00044